D0875986

THE AUDIO-TUTORIAL
SYSTEM

The Instructional Design Library

Volume 3

THE AUDIO-TUTORIAL SYSTEM

James D. Russell
Department of Education
Purdue University
West Lafayette, Indiana

Danny G. Langdon
Series Editor

Educational Technology Publications
Englewood Cliffs, New Jersey 07632

GALLAUDET COLLEGE LIBRARY
WASHINGTON, D. C.

Library of Congress Cataloging in Publication Data

Russell, James D
    The audio-tutorial system.

    (The Instructional design library; v. no. 3)
    Bibliography: p.
    1. Independent study. 2. Audio-visual
education. 3. Programmed instruction. I. Title.
II. Series.
LB1049.R88   371.39'4   77-25454
ISBN 0-87778-107-9

Copyright © 1978 Educational Technology Publications, Inc., Englewood Cliffs, New Jersey 07632.

All rights reserved. No part of this book may be reproduced or transmitted, in any form or by any means, electronic or mechanical, including photocopying, recording, or by any information storage and retrieval system without permission in writing from the Publisher.

Printed in the United States of America.

Library of Congress Catalog Card Number:
77-25454.

International Standard Book Number:
0-87778-107-9.

First Printing: February, 1978.

371.39
R8a
1978

FOREWORD

Many years ago, when I was just a novice to the field of Instructional Technology and trying to write my first objectives, an "experienced" colleague handed me a three-page copy of something called "How to Prepare an Audio-Tutorial Lesson." This is my way of saying that the Audio-Tutorial System has been around long enough to have withstood the test of time. Certainly, enough courses, programs, and evaluation studies have been done to conclude that this instructional design has merit in producing learning.

Dr. James Russell has done a splendid job of distilling and illustrating the essential features of the Audio-Tutorial System. In reading what Dr. Russell has to say, you must "keep your eye on the ball." Audio is not used in this case as a lecture on tape, but as both a guiding function for tutoring and a facilitating function for helping the student learn. It takes some developmental time, effort, and money to put this system into operation, but dividends are paid again and again.

Danny G. Langdon
Series Editor

211400

PREFACE

First and foremost, I want to thank Sam Postlethwait, who directly or indirectly taught me everything I know about the Audio-Tutorial approach. One of the highlights of my professional career was to work closely with Dr. Postlethwait for several years. Since then we have been associated in numerous projects and workshops.

The sample lesson included in this monograph was designed and developed by Dr. Howard Russock. I certainly appreciate his willingness to let me include it. In addition, I am indebted to Drs. Kathleen M. Fisher and Brian Mac Whinney for an excellent review of Audio-Tutorial research which served as a basis for the section on "Outcomes."

I wish I could acknowledge everyone who read the tryout version of this book. Each and every reaction was taken into consideration when finalizing the volume. Thanks to all who contributed—students, workshop participants, faculty, and colleagues.

Finally, I want to acknowledge the valuable assistance of Danny Langdon, the Series Editor, who made this work possible. He conceived the idea for the Series—inviting me to prepare these materials—and provided a very critical and helpful review of the original manuscript.

You, the reader, are why it was written. If you have any questions or need additional information, please contact me at the address given in the Resources section at the end of the book.

J.D.R.

CONTENTS

ABSTRACT

THE AUDIO-TUTORIAL SYSTEM

The Audio-Tutorial System, initiated by S.N. Postelthwait at Purdue University in 1961, has evolved from use in a single botany course to a concept presently being used by thousands of teachers at all levels of instruction, from kindergarten through graduate school; and in all major subject fields, including business, industry, and the military. The approach allows the teacher to individualize instruction for his or her students while actively involving them in the learning process. One of Dr. Postlethwait's principles is: "Learning must be done by the learner."

Media and group size are selected and used on the basis of their effectiveness and benefit to the students, not their convenience for the teacher. Activities best handled with a large group take place in the General Assembly Session (GAS). Student-to-student interactions and small-group discussions are an integral part of the Small Assembly Session (SAS). Study by the individual student, and student-teacher interaction are provided for during the Independent Study Session (ISS). During the ISS, the student's learning activities are directed by an audio tape which stimulates a tutorial session with the instructor; hence, the name Audio-Tutorial.

There is not a single Audio-Tutorial System; rather, it is a systematic approach to enhance and facilitate learning. The teacher must adapt the approach to his subject matter.

Research shows that the A-T method has been used effectively in a broad range of disciplines with students of all ages.

THE AUDIO-TUTORIAL
SYSTEM

I.

USE

Introduction to the Audio-Tutorial System

Individual students respond differently to various learning activities, media, and rates of learning. The Audio-Tutorial System provides a multi-faceted, multi-media approach to learning which is under the control of the student. It utilizes an *audio* tape as a programming device to *tutor* the student through the instructional activities and media until he has mastered the objectives of the lesson. The Audio-Tutorial approach is a total instructional system composed of the following three basic components:

Independent Study Session. During a typical session, the student is actively involved in learning at his own pace. He listens, reads, writes, manipulates learning materials, makes observations, and performs experiments. This component of the Audio-Tutorial approach is designed to help the student master the objectives. If the student has difficulty learning the material, he may replay the tape as often as necessary or discuss his questions with an instructor on duty in the learning center. As the name implies, the student studies independently in a learning carrel. Each student is usually free to begin or end the study session whenever he or she chooses.

General Assembly Session. Some instructional activities are best handled in a large-group session. The General Assembly

Session may be used for orientation to the course content, to present guest lecturers, or to show films. It may also provide motivation, enrichment, preview, or review. Hourly examinations can be given during the scheduled large group session.

Small Assembly Session. Evaluation of the students' learning is handled in a modified seminar, which includes both an oral and a written quiz. Six or eight students sit informally around a table with an instructor. The various items and instructional materials which were used in the Independent Study Session serve as a basis for student discussions. The objectives for the lesson are randomly assigned to the students one at a time. The student then demonstrates the performance called for by that objective. The student's performance is evaluated and then the other students each have an opportunity to make comments, corrections, or additions to what was said. The oral quiz session is followed by a short written quiz. The Small Assembly Session is an effective feedback mechanism for checking the success or failure of the students as well as the quality of the Audio-Tutorial lesson itself. The quiz session can provide clues for improving the instructional materials and activities. The Small Assembly Session employs the principle that "one really learns only when one teaches." In this session each student is in effect a teacher as he makes his oral presentation.

Probably the greatest advantage of the Audio-Tutorial System is the flexibility which it offers both the student and the teacher. The instructor may select multi-media instructional materials to organize and present course content for a totally integrated approach to learning. Also, the content can be organized and presented in a variety of ways to facilitate learning. Its flexibility allows the student to proceed at his own pace and to achieve regardless of his background, aptitude, and interests. The student can also study at the time most convenient for him.

When evaluating the system using student achievement, it has been demonstrated that students tend to learn at a faster rate under the Audio-Tutorial System than in the lecture method. Some studies comparing the Audio-Tutorial System with more conventional instruction have shown that students learn more in the same time using A-T. Other studies have demonstrated that students learn the same amount of material in less time using A-T. One study even indicated that the A-T students spent half as much time to master the same objectives. An additional factor favoring the Audio-Tutorial System is that most students prefer this system of instruction over more conventional modes.

The emphasis of the Audio-Tutorial System is on students learning rather than the instructor teaching. The student can manipulate the actual learning materials rather than having them under the control of the teacher. The focus is on the student. The system is an attempt to actively involve the student in the learning process. The system combines the more conventional lecture and laboratory into an integrated learning experience. The experience may utilize a variety of components including tangibles (real objects), printed materials (textbooks, journal articles, etc.), audio (tutorial discussion, sound effects, etc.), projected media (films, slides) and human interaction (student-student and student-teacher).

Another advantage of the Audio-Tutorial System is its emphasis on the student's self-reliance and independence in learning. It places the responsibility for learning squarely on the shoulders of the student. A consequence is that the student learns how to learn. One purpose of any educational system should be to release the student from his dependence upon the teacher for learning. The Audio-Tutorial System promotes this independence.

Since the content of the Audio-Tutorial lesson is open for examination by colleagues, the instructor is "forced" to present his best product and not to merely "get by" with a lecture that was hastily prepared just before a class meeting.

The only really serious disadvantage of the Audio-Tutorial System is the expense involved in setting up and maintaining the system—both in time and money. The initial investment in hardware need not be extravagant. However, the real investment comes in the development of software, since very little material is commercially available at the present time. The man-hours required to produce material for one hour of student time vary from a few hours to several hundred hours, depending upon the subject matter and the quality of the final product. Many people feel it is more difficult to develop an Audio-Tutorial lesson than it is to prepare a more conventional lecture-laboratory sequence.

Critics of the system have stated that the tape recorder causes mechanization of learning and results in de-humanization of instruction. Actually, since the teacher does not have to lecture, there is more time for interacting with students. An instructor should always be available during the Independent Study Session to answer questions. The nature of the Small Assembly Session provides for more personal interaction during the evaluation process.

Teachers seem to have greater difficulty adjusting to the Audio-Tutorial System than do students. Some teachers prefer the role of lecturer and are uncomfortable in the one-to-one interaction with students.

Even though the Audio-Tutorial approach to instruction can be used to teach anything to anybody, utilization of A-T seems particularly suitable for introductory courses having high fact/principle content and large numbers of students. The system is a real asset when the students are non-homogeneous (i.e., having a varied background, wide achievement levels, and diverse needs and interests).

The System has a very broad range of applications. It has been applied successfully with all ages and at all grade levels, from preschool to post-doctoral studies. The use of audio materials is particularly appropriate for preschool and early elementary students, who have not perfected their reading skills. In addition to more traditional educational applications, the A-T approach has been used in job-related learning for business, industry, and the military. It not only provides for individualized learning through independent study, but also combines large-group, small-group, and independent study into a total learning system.

Even though the System is applicable in all subject matter fields, the most frequent use seems to be in the science area and especially biology (botany), perhaps since that is where A-T got its start. It is also possible to use the System for all types of learning—cognitive (knowledge), psychomotor (manipulative skills), and affective (attitudes). Affective learning is particularly enhanced by the General Assembly Session and the Small Assembly Session.

Of course, A-T can be used with any number of students, but it becomes more feasible and efficient as the number of students increases. Most users of the system feel that 30 tends to be the minimum number for use of the System. With fewer than 30, it is easier to use other, more traditional approaches to instruction. The largest Audio-Tutorial System known to the author is the Introduction to Biology course at The Ohio State University, which serves about 4,000 students per quarter or 12,000 per year.

The Audio-Tutorial System was first used in 1961 by Dr. S.N. "Sam" Postlethwait in an introductory botany course at Purdue University. Someone seeing the name "Audio-Tutorial" for the first time usually puts the emphasis on "Audio"and conceives of the system as a lecture on tape. Unfortunately, this was not Dr. Postlethwait's intention. The emphasis properly belongs on "Tutorial," since Dr. Postlethwait conceived the approach in order to provide individualized (i.e., tutorial) instruction for a larger number of students than a single teacher could interact with on a true one-to-one basis. It was Dr. Postlethwait's desire to *help students learn*, and he found that he could use an audio tape to meaningfully tutor individual students through a series of learning activities.

II.

OPERATIONAL DESCRIPTION

An Overview of the A-T System

The Audio-Tutorial approach is a *system*. Like other systems, it is composed of component parts or subsystems. Since traditionally the terms lecture, laboratory, and recitation denote an emphasis on teaching, the A-T Approach uses General Assembly Session, Independent Study Session, and Small Assembly Session, thereby putting the rightful emphasis on learning. Thus, the three basic components of the A-T system are:

General Assembly Session (GAS)

Independent Study Session (ISS)

Small Assembly Session (SAS)

Even though the components of the system can be arranged in any sequence, depending upon the nature of the subject matter, the judgment of the instructor, the availability of the students, and facilities, Dr. Postlethwait's original sequence is still used by many A-T instructors. To illustrate this sequence, study begins with the General Assembly Session to orient the students to the unit of study, typically a week's work. The GAS is followed by the Independent Study Session, in which the student studies the content of the lesson at his own pace. Finally, the Small Assembly Session is used to evaluate each student's mastery of the objectives outlined in the unit of study.

General Assembly Session

The General Assembly Session can be similar in nature to a conventional lecture session or used as creatively as the instructor wishes. Attendance may or may not be required. Instructors may have some required sessions, other sessions that are highly recommended, and still others that are optional. Most importantly, the GAS should be operated on a flexible basis to meet the needs of the students.

The General Assembly Session should be used for those activities that are best done with a large group of students (30 to 100 or more). Such activities include lectures, guest speakers, showing films or videotapes, and examinations. The GAS can be used for motivation and to provide an introduction or orientation and rationale for a week's study. If different learning sequences are used with different students, the GAS becomes important and more difficult to manage. The author has observed that it is being used less today than previously.

Independent Study Session

The heart of the A-T System is the Independent Study Session (ISS). As the title suggests, the student studies at his own time and pace, but *not* without the assistance of a qualified instructor who is available when needed. The ISS typically takes place in a learning center equipped with study carrels. However, it should be pointed out that carrels are *not* a critical requirement. The critical requirements do include a relatively quiet and comfortable environment where the student can concentrate, and have access to the necessary equipment and the space to manipulate the materials. Hence, it could be a corner of a classroom or library! An audio tape playback unit is required, but it need not have recording capabilities. As indicated earlier, individual assistance with questions about the subject matter should always be available when needed. Of course, additional equipment will be needed if slides, films, or video tapes are used in a multi-media approach.

Usually the learning center is open a number of hours during the day (and night for community colleges and universities). The Independent Study Session is scheduled to accommodate the number of students in the course and the average amount of time that they are expected to spend in the learning center. On the elementary and secondary level these times are usually individually pre-scheduled, although a student is often permitted to come to the learning center during his study hall if his presence does not disrupt the other students scheduled at that time. At the junior college and university level, the "barber shop" approach is often used—first come, first served. This may create a waiting line at the more ideal times. The problem may be alleviated by scheduling the students into the learning center, but this also eliminates the freedom of the student to "come and go" and study as allowed by his own class-work schedule. One creative approach used by Dr. Postlethwait is to post a past record of the number of students in the learning center at hourly intervals. This enables the students to acknowledge the busy times and arrange to come at other less-crowded times. Some schools have compromised and have scheduled students during part of the ISS. For example, two hours scheduled and another one or two hours to be arranged. Other instructors let students earn the right for independence by scheduling all students at the beginning of the semester, and those students who perform satisfactorily earn the right to come at times other than those scheduled.

It can not be over-stressed that during the ISS, emphasis is on student learning rather than on the teacher's teaching. Objectives are provided to the student when he comes to the learning center, and each student is aware of his responsponsibility to master the objectives. The student is guided by the audio tape as he proceeds through the lesson. However, since he has the objectives, he may elect to design his own learning strategies and sequence. The main concern of both the student and the teacher should be that each student demonstrates competence to a pre-established level on each of the objectives.

Role of the Audio Tape

The Audio-Tutorial approach must not be confused with a "lecture on tape." Rather, the audio tape is a device for programming each individual student through the learning sequences. The student is vicariously "tutored" by the instructor, and the student controls the rate at which he proceeds with his study. There should be no attempt to substitute audio input from the teacher for reading, performing an experiment, solving a problem, etc. These are all meaningful experiences through which the student learns by "doing." Further, some modern media (i.e., television and computers) have been used as the only source of information or medium of communication. Learning by its very nature is a multi-sensory task, and individual students require different "mixes" of sensory inputs for mastery. The guideline in designing A-T lessons should be to use a wide variety of media, with the audio tape only as a guide.

Along with the audio tape as a guide and an instructor as a resource person, the student typically has available in the learning center his own copy of the study guide, which contains key points from the lesson, exercises to complete, problems to solve, as well as a place to make additional notes. In addition, actual objects (plants, rocks, or whatever relates to the topic), color slides, and displays are provided to enhance the students' learning.

The ISS is based upon the premise that learning must be done by the learner and that all study activities should involve the learner as actively as possible. As Dr. Postlethwait says, "Learning is an activity done *by* an individual not something done *to* an individual."

When the student has mastered the objects to his satisfaction, he replaces the study materials where he found them and arranges the learning carrel as it was when he started the lesson. Often a self-check is included in the study guide to allow the student to practice the objectives and determine if he or she has learned the materials. The self-check questions are similar to the questions which will be used for evaluation of the lesson later.

Small Assembly Session

The small assembly session (SAS) is a group of six to ten students sitting down with an instructor. This type of session may be used for "recitation," group discussion, oral evaluation, or to plan a group project or activity.

When the small-group session is used primarily for evaluation, it is often called an "Integrated Quiz Session" (IQS), since it attempts to integrate via evaluation techniques and knowledge the students' learning for that week. (The students refer to it as an "IQ Session.") The IQS follows the students' study of a prescribed number of A-T units, and it is usually scheduled for 30 to 60 minutes.

The instructor randomly assigns students to demonstrate their competence of the stated objectives for the lesson(s) being evaluated. The students, in turn, discuss or do what the objectives require, compare "democracy" and "monarchy," identify the parts of a microscope with a microscope in hand, or measure the thickness of a piece of metal to the nearest one thousandth of an inch with a micrometer.

If the objectives for the lesson are in a hierarchical sequence, where one depends upon those which precede it, then the instructor usually covers the objectives in sequence and randomly chooses the students. If the instructor goes around the table in order, the next student will be thinking through his response to the upcoming objective and not be attending to the objective being discussed. When the objectives are not in a hierarchical sequence, the author has found that playing cards can be used to assign the objectives to the students. Often there are less than ten objectives, so the appropriate number of cards are placed in the center of the table, e.g., ace through ten of clubs. If there are more than ten objectives, then the first ten objectives might correspond to the ace through ten of clubs and the next ten objectives (11 through 20), could correspond to the hearts (ace through ten), etc. The necessary cards, corresponding to the number of objectives, are shuffled and placed in the center of the table. The student who plans to discuss an objective first draws a card from the pile. When he is finished, the next student draws a card and does that objective until everyone has had a turn. To add a little excitement to the activity an occasional "wild card" or joker is mixed into the pile and the person who draws it gets an automatic perfect score without having to discuss any objective!

The purpose of this approach is to encourage each student to prepare to discuss all the objectives. The technique is based upon the idea that "you really learn something when you have to teach it to somebody else." So each student is expected to prepare a "mini-lecture" or short presentation on all the objectives. After the student completes his presentation on the assigned objective, other students have an opportunity to add to or correct what the student has said. Students who make valuable additional comments may receive a couple of bonus points.

Since each student usually discusses only one objective during the IQS, most instructors want to evaluate his or her competence on other objectives as well, and this can be done using a written quiz. The written quizzes should measure objective mastery. They may be true-false, matching, short answer, or essay.

Overall, the Small Assembly Session is very effective for reviewing important content, providing reinforcement for correct learning, clarifying misconceptions, giving feedback to both students and instructor, and establishing rapport with the students.

Additional Activities

Some instructional activities do not conveniently fit into a large-group presentation, a small-group discussion, or independent study in a learning center. However, any activity can be programmed into the total Audio-Tutorial System. For example, conventional field trips can be added to the study program. The portable tape recorder can be used for an individual field trip around the campus, nature area, or museum.

To incorporate several portions of different lessons, to analyze or to apply principles and techniques learned in a course, many instructors use term projects and/or scientific research projects along with special reading assignments in journals.

Dr. Postlethwait raises the question, "What procedure would you use to teach a friend botany (or a subject of your choice)?" It is unlikely the answer would be "two lectures, a recitation, and a three-hour laboratory each week for a semester." Dr. Postlethwait contends: "It is more likely that you would meet with this friend at a mutually convenient time with the materials available which are useful in helping him learn botany (or your subject), and would then tutor him through a series of learning events. There would be a one-to-one relationship and the student would be involved in the program at all times." Realizing that this approach is not feasible with a large number of students, Dr. Postlethwait designed the Audio-Tutorial System to simulate this relationship for an unlimited number of students. As he describes it: "The appropriate materials can be collected and the instructor can sit among them talking into a tape recorder as if he were instructing one individual. The arrangement of materials and the resultant tape can be duplicated as many times as required for the number of students involved. In this way hundreds can have the benefit of personalized instruction by a competent and knowledgeable instructor. The program can be tested and revised until it produces consistent and satisfactory results. In addition, the student can participate in adjusting the program to his background, interest, and capacity."

Advantages

There are numerous advantages of the Audio-Tutorial approach over other instructional strategies; however, none of these advantages are unique to A-T. Since A-T is a total system the advantages of a variety of instructional techniques are inherent. For instance, freedom and flexibility are advantageous characteristics of the system. The teacher is free to do, within the approach, anything that will enhance student learning. The student is free to choose from among a variety of approaches that which best fits his learning style. As Dr. Postlethwait has pointed out frequently, "on his way to class a student can stop at an ordinary vending machine and select four different types of coffee—black, cream, sugar, or cream and sugar. However, when this same student enters the classroom, he is often forced to receive the same instruction as several hundred other students." As was pointed out earlier, students differ greatly in ways other than their taste for coffee. They enter courses with different achievement levels, a wide variety of interests and needs, and different learning styles. A-T lessons can be selected and sequenced in a variety of ways to accommodate a variety of needs, interests, abilities, and backgrounds.

The rate and intensity of study is under the control of the student and not paced by the teacher. He can stop the self-study units at any time to repeat what has just been presented, skip ahead, get assistance from a peer or instructor, or just take a break. Consequently, redundancy can be reduced within the audio presentation, and the most efficient use can be made of the student's time. He can provide redundancy if necessary by going back and listening to a portion of the tape a second, third, or fourth time. The tape player is a very patient tutor.

The system is designed to provide the opportunity for large-group instruction where it is most efficient and effective. The same is true for small-group discussions. The Independent Study Session has the advantage of a tutorial session which actively involves the student in learning. Selection of materials and student activities are limited only by the imagination and creativity of the instructor.

One of the most important advantages of the system is that the entire A-T approach is designed for success. The instructor should expect that given the proper directions and the necessary time to study, a majority of the students will be able to master a majority of the objectives for each A-T lesson.

Disadvantages

The emphasis of the A-T system is on student learning rather than the teacher teaching; therefore, the major responsibility for learning must rest squarely on the shoulders of the student. However, this can lead to the biggest disadvantage of the system, from the author's point of view, and that is procrastination.

As Dr. Postlethwait says: "Students are a lot like people!" Therefore, the teacher must motivate the student to spend the time he or she needs to learn the material. The teacher can enforce rigid deadlines or require a certain amount of work per unit time; however, this defeats many of the advantages of the system. It is sometimes difficult for the teacher to differentiate between students who are having genuine difficulty and those who are procrastinating.

The teacher must also be willing to change his role. He is no longer a direct disseminator of information in the A-T System. After the individual lessons have been designed and put on tape, the teacher becomes a resource person, counselor, and evaluator. The teacher must also adjust to having his efforts and objectives exposed to students and colleagues for review and criticism. However, conscientious educators rarely shy away from accountability.

It should be pointed out that there is nothing wrong with a good classroom presentation. In fact, lectures are an integral part of the Audio-Tutorial System. However, teaching is more than dispensing information. Accordingly, the role of the teacher should involve more than presenting information in a lecture format. This function can be handled by printed materials and audio-video tapes. A more creative and challenging role of the teacher should be that of "director of learning" rather than disseminator of information. In the Audio-Tutorial System, most of the factual information is acquired by the student through reading and in the Independent Study Session. However, learning activities may include: writing a one-act play, performing experiments, building a model, viewing short films, dissecting specimens, and any other study activity deemed helpful by the teacher or the student. The A-T approach differentiates between "being told the facts" and learning.

Being relieved of the job of "information transfer," the teacher can tackle the more dynamic roles of *diagnostician, resource person*, and *motivator*. In the Audio-Tutorial System, the teaching staff should be ready, willing, and able to serve any of these functions (and others) at any time. However, the three functions listed tend to be associated with the three components of the system. The teacher's role of diagnostician is most closely associated with the Small Assembly Session, particularly when it is used for evaluative purposes. Seeing the student in action as he describes the objectives and demonstrates his understanding of the material, the teacher is in an excellent position to diagnose difficulties which individual students might be having with the course. At the same time, he may be observing common problems which might be attributed to the learning materials. His role of resource person might be carried out in his office when the student has a question, on the telephone, or in the hallway between classes. However, it is most likely to be needed in the Independent Study Session, when the student encounters difficulty during his initial study of the material. As mentioned earlier, there should be someone available to answer student questions whenever the Learning Center is open. One of the main purposes of the General Assembly Session, as used by most instructors, is motivation, to provide an introduction to the material under study and to provide a rationale for the importance of studying the material.

Comparison of Conventional and Audio-Tutorial Courses

The question is often asked, "How is Audio-Tutorial instruction actually different from conventional instruction?" Previously, it was pointed out that the A-T components of General Assembly Session, Independent Study Session, and

Small Assembly Session could be analogous to the lecture, laboratory, recitation experiences usually found in the classroom. What, then, makes A-T unique? What sets A-T apart from customary classroom procedure? In an attempt to answer this question, Postlethwait and Russell (1971) devised the following comparison table. It should be pointed out that some of the characteristics attributed to Audio-Tutorial instruction are found in traditional courses. In many cases these characteristics are an example of positive influences of the A-T approach on traditional instruction. Then, too, all A-T programs do not exhibit all the characteristics contained in the chart. The chart is for comparative purposes only, and it is not meant to rigidly define either conventional or Audio-Tutorial instruction. The descriptions tend to be the extemes.

Conventional Courses	CHARACTERISTIC	Audio-Tutorial Courses
	LEARNING EXPERIENCES	
Conventional courses are usually characterized by lectures, reading the text, group discussions, and sometimes related laboratory experiences. The learning experiences are oriented toward teacher performance and group instruction with emphasis on teaching.		A-T courses provide for a combination of learning experiences with an integrated sequence so that each learning activity enhances and complements the others. The learning experiences are oriented toward student performance and individual instruction with emphasis on learning.
	OBJECTIVES	
Objectives are *not* usually stated in specific, behavioral terms. They may be inferred from the content of the subject matter and tests.		Objectives are stated in terms of student performance and given to the student before the instruction begins.
	INSTRUCTIONAL MATERIALS	
Materials (texts, films, etc.) are selected first, and tests are designed to sample this material, but		Objectives are stated first, test items are designed to measure mastery of these objectives, then

Conventional Courses   **Audio-Tutorial Courses**

INSTRUCTIONAL MATERIALS (Continued)

desired behavior with respect to the materials is not usually defined in advance.

instructional materials are selected to assist the student in mastering the objectives.

RATE

Students are forced to go through the instruction in a "lockstep manner" (all going at the *same* rate.) They begin at the same time and are expected to finish simultaneously.

Each student can proceed at his own rate. He is free to skip any portion of the A-T lesson as long as he can demonstrate mastery of the objectives. He can also repeat any portion of the lesson.

STRATEGIES AND MEDIA

Teachers tend to use one or two strategies, such as lecture and written assignments, regardless of what the student is expected to learn. Media (usually printed) are prepared and used on the basis of the teacher's feeling comfortable with it.

Different learning strategies are used for objectives representing different kinds of learning. A variety of instructional strategies is used to optimize learning on a given topic. Media are selected to complement the type of objective and characteristics of the students.

INDIVIDUALIZATION

Conventional courses are group-oriented. Students are usually provided with a limited number of instructional resources. Usually the teacher specifies exactly how the student should proceed—read 20 pages of the text and answer 10 questions, etc.

A-T Systems are highly individualized. Each student can use any or all of the media and materials available. The selection of the most appropriate approach is often left to the student—listen to a tape, read a text, look at diagrams, view a film, examine real objects, or any combination thereof.

ROLE OF STUDENT

The student's role is usually passive—reading the text or just listening to the teacher.

A-T provides for active student participation. The student learns by doing. The student is actively involved in manipulating the instructional materials.

Conventional Courses	Audio-Tutorial Courses

TIME

Time spent on a topic is usually constant for all learners, resulting in no time variance; thus, achievement scores correlate highly with I.Q. | The students spend as much time as necessary to master the topic. Time required for mastery tends to correlate highly with I.Q.

FREEDOM

Traditionally 45 minutes or an hour each day are scheduled at a fixed time for instruction. Students are forced to attend lectures and laboratories (e.g. from 8:00 to 8:50 on Monday, Wednesday, and Friday). | Instruction can be at the student's convenience and at the time of day when the student learns "best." A-T provides greater freedom for students to adjust study time and subject matter content to individual needs and peculiarities of interest.

TESTING

Tests usually sample the content which has been "covered." The student is often at a loss as to how to prepare (study) for the test. The student sits through the course, then takes an examination to determine his grade for the course. Tests are too often used only to "give grades," rather than for feedback or diagnosis. | Learners are given the objectives and told how attainment of them will be evaluated. Tests are designed to measure mastery of the objectives. The student receives credit when he can demonstrate mastery, even if he has *not* gone through the A-T lesson. Test items (questions) are used for assessing prerequisite skills, for diagnosing difficulties, and for confirming mastery.

PORTABILITY

Conventional courses are usually based upon the teacher's lecture and are only portable by moving the teacher to a new location (sometimes accomplished via videotape). The lecture is usually lost forever once the class period ends. If a student misses part of a conventional course, he must talk with the teacher, review a fellow | A-T units are portable and can be available at a variety of locations —in the field, at home, in a hospital, etc. Since the units are separate, make-up lessons can be accommodated with a minimum of effort. All students are exposed to the same instruction, regardless of the hour of the day or the day of the week.

Conventional Courses   **Audio-Tutorial Courses**

PORTABILITY (Continued)

student's notes or miss the instruction entirely.

FLEXIBILITY

Conventional courses are struc-	A-T systems can be structured
tured around a semester or year-	into a greater variety of patterns
long study guide or textbook and	consistent with different ap-
tend to be relatively inflexible.	proaches or themes.

COURSE SUCCESS

Lacking the features of systematic	Having a design goal and an evalu-
design and specific objectives,	ation plan, the instructor can cor-
there is no built-in provision for	rect faulty instructional materials,
judging success of the course oth-	and realize when he has succeeded
er than the teacher's subjective	in developing a successful course.
opinion.	

References
(OPERATIONAL DESCRIPTION section)

Postlethwait, S.N. and J.D. Russell. "Minicourses"—The Style
of the Future. In J.G. Creager and D.L. Murray
(Eds.), *The Use of Modules in College Biology Teaching.*
Washington, D.C.: The American Institute of Biological
Sciences, 1971.

III.

DESIGN FORMAT

A Sample A-T Lesson

In order to give you the feeling of an Audio-Tutorial lesson, an excerpt from a unit by Dr. Howard I. Russock* is described in this section. Dr. Russock designed this A-T lesson on "Personal Space" for use in introductory courses for general biology, zoology, and psychology. As you read the transcript of the audio tape, view the study guide reproduced, and see pictures of the displays, you must realize that the printed format is a poor substitute for the real sights and sounds that make up the actual A-T learning experience.

You enter the learning center and sit down at a booth (see Figure 1.). There you have a study guide, audio tape, and film. The other materials are located on a display table near the middle of the learning center. Before you begin, you read the summary, rationale, and objectives for the lesson on personal space (see Figure 2.). The objectives let you know the key points to learn from the lesson. Now position your head phones, start the tape player and hear:

On display in the Learning Center you'll find a cage full of rodents and an aquarium with fish in it. Why don't you take a look at the fish and rodents and especially notice the way

*Howard Russock received his Ph.D. in Biology from West Virginia University and is presently Assistant Professor of Biology and Environmental Science at Western Connecticut State College.

Figure 1

A Learning Carrel

*that they space themselves in their environment? Under
Exercise 1 on page 1 in your Study Guide you can record
your thoughts on the ways these animals space themselves.
MUSIC.*

You then get up from the booth and go to the display table
and view the rodents and fish (not shown here). After

Figure 2

*Introductory Page from Study Guide
on "Personal Space"*

Summary
This mini-course will involve you in a brief study of the concept of *personal space* and the relevancy of personal space to humans. The term refers to the normal spacing that animals maintain between themselves and their fellows. This distance acts as an invisible bubble that surrounds the organism. Violating the personal space of an animal may produce major changes in the behavior of the animal involved.

Rationale
The study of how living organisms use and organize the space around them is important to the understanding of animal behavior and social structure. It is also important to the understanding of our own reactions to crowding and physical contact, the behavioral similarities between humans and other animals, and to the study of human behavior in general.

Objectives
Upon completion of this mini-course you will be able to:
1. Define personal space.
2. Describe three specific examples of personal space in animals and recognize examples of personal space from a series of pictures.
3. Describe a situation in which animals exhibit a constant personal space.
4. Define and distinguish between flight distance, defense distance, and personal space.
5. Predict what may happen if the personal space of a particular animal is violated (under a specific set of circumstances).
6. Describe four situations in which the personal space of an animal is very small or non-existent.
7. Using data from personal experimentation, cite evidence for the existence of personal space in humans.
8. Describe two situations in which humans exhibit personal space.
9. Describe from personal experience what happens when the personal space of a human is violated and compare these events to the violation of personal space in other animals.
10. Compare the size of the personal space of individuals of different genders and cultures (using data from personal experimentation).

viewing these creatures as long as you care to, you record
the response to exercise 1 in your study guide shown below:

1

I. HOW DO ANIMALS SPACE THEMSELVES:

Exercise 1. How do fish and rodents differ in the way they space
themselves in their environment?

After completing exercise 1, you return to the carrel and
continue with the tape:

*Okay, did you find that the fish rarely, if ever, touch
each other? How about the rodents? Well, they were probably constantly touching one another—they may have been
sleeping in a heap—but in any case, they often touched.
This minicourse is an investigation of the way that animals
space themselves. We're going to be particularly interested
in the question of what personal space is, and how personal
space helps animals regulate their societies.*

*All right, let's get started. What are the characteristics
of personal space? Will you look at Slide 1? (See Figure 3.)
These birds seem to be a fairly constant distance apart,
don't they? Why don't you pick up your ruler and actually
measure how far apart these birds appear on the slide? It
doesn't really matter what part of the bird you measure
from, as long as you are consistent for all the birds. After you
measure these relative distances you can record them in your
Study Guide under Exercise 2 on page 2. MUSIC.*

Figure 3

Photograph Used in Lesson

The music signals the student to turn off the tape player, pick up the ruler, and get actively involved in the lesson. When he has completed the activity, he returns to the tape.

Well, did you find that the spacing between those birds was fairly constant? Of course, the space between each of the birds was not exactly the same. This is partially because of minor individual variation in the birds, or perhaps due to distortion in the photograph. But I think that you can see that in a given situation, many species tend to maintain a fairly constant distance between themselves. In other words, a fairly constant personal space between themselves. If you want to further verify this conclusion for yourself, I suggest that the next time you have an opportunity that you observe a large school of fish, or a flock of birds flying South in the fall, or perhaps a group of birds of the same species just sitting on a wire. If you look closely you will see that these animals are maintaining a fairly constant space between themselves in all of these different situations.

Okay, now would you take a look at Exercise 3 on page 3? Another question that might be occurring to you is, what happens when the personal space of an animal is violated by another animal of its species? At this point, I'd like you to do something fairly unusual. Would you get up from your seat and stand very close, unusually close, to some other person in the Learning Center? Some person who is doing some other minicourse. While you're standing there observe how this person reacts to you. You can write down your observation under Exercise 3. MUSIC.

3
Exercise 3. What happened when you stood "abnormally" close to another person? (Did (s)he look 'uneasy,' move away from you, look at you as if you were strange, hit you, kiss you, or do something else?)

Well, what happened? I could guess that that person you stood next to probably looked rather uneasy. He might have moved his chair away from you; he may have looked at you as though you were somewhat strange; and if you were really unlucky you might have been attacked. However, this outcome is rare enough that I felt safe in including the exercise in the Study Guide. In any case, it appears that humans may react several ways to a violation of personal space.

How do you think other animals react when their personal space is violated? Unfortunately, we can't bring animals into the Learning Center to show you what happens when their personal space is violated. Animals just don't act very naturally in the laboratory. But I do have a film loop. This film loop was originally made for another purpose and it deals in general with chicken behavior, but the vast majority of the film loop deals with paired encounters of chickens, and in each case one of the chickens comes very close to another chicken and violates its personal space. Why don't you look at the film loop, and then write down what actually does happen when a chicken's personal space is violated? MUSIC.

Here we see another form of media used—the 8mm film loop. The student can look at the film as long as he desires. As indicated the film used is one commercially produced but fits very well into this Audio-Tutorial lesson. After viewing the film loop, the student returns to the tape:

Well, did you find that several things may happen when the personal space of an animal is violated? One thing that may happen is that the animals fight. In several other cases one of the animals simply backs off. In other cases the animals don't really seem to be doing much of anything at all, although we might say, subjectively, that the chickens involved seem to be somewhat nervous or ill-at-ease. The way a particular animal reacts to a violation of its personal space really depends on many factors. The most important of these factors may be the animal's position in its particular social group.

The A-T lesson goes on to introduce the concepts of flight distance and defense distance. Slides are used to show several examples of animals violating personal space without violence in such cases as mating, nursing, feeding, playing, and grooming. The student then leaves the carrel to perform some experiments designed to answer the question of whether or not humans exhibit personal space. One of the experiments is reproduced in Figure 4.

Figure 4

A. Do humans exhibit personal space?

EXPERIMENT 1
(adapted from Barash, 1975)*

Subject and Materials
This field study can be conducted almost anywhere. Your work will involve both observation and simple experiments. The reading room of a university library is an ideal study site, and will be assumed as the locale of the following investigation, although with minor adjustments cafeterias, restaurants, park benches, theaters and buses may be substituted. A watch with a sweep second hand is the only necessary equipment.

Procedure
First, construct a map of the seating area of the location you have chosen, showing the placement of tables and the number of individuals at each table. Then, over a period of 30-60 minutes record the percentage of tables that are occupied by at least one person before incoming people begin sitting at already occupied tables. When incoming people do begin sitting at occupied tables, record the percentage of people sitting down
(a)   directly across from the person already at the table
(b)   adjacent to the person already at the table
(c)   diagonally across from the person already at the table

Note: Ignore people who sit down at an occupied table because they obviously know the occupant.
(1)   What percentage of the tables have to be occupied before new, incoming people start sitting at occupied tables?
(2)   When new people do start sitting at occupied tables, do they most often prefer to sit directly across from, adjacent to, or diagonally across from the occupants? When the preferred seat is taken, where do incoming people sit next?
(3)   What do these results tell you about personal space in humans?

*Barash, D. P. "Human Ethology and the Concept of Personal Space." In *Animal Behavior in Laboratory and Field*, 2nd ed. E. O. Price and A. W. Stokes (Eds.) San Francisco: Freeman, 1975, p. 128.

Figure 5

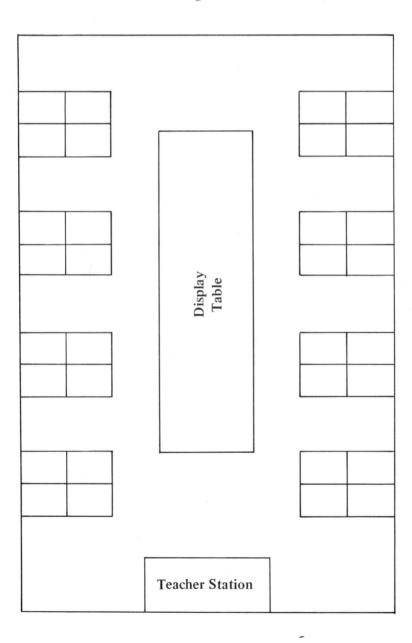

have 50 students using the learning center an average of four hours per week per student and the learning center is open four hours a day Monday through Friday, how many carrels should you have?

$$\text{Students} \times \frac{\text{Avg. Hrs/Wk}}{\text{Student}} = \text{No. of Booths} \times \frac{\text{Hours Open}}{\text{Week}}$$

$$50 \quad \times \quad 4 \quad = \quad ? \quad \times 20 \text{ (4 hrs. M-F)}$$

$$200 \quad = \quad 20 \quad \times \text{No. of Booths}$$

$$10 \quad = \text{No. of Booths}$$

Of course, ten would be the bare minimum. You should either plan for an extra booth or have some extra time available, since there will unlikely be 100 percent efficiency in the use of the booths. Obviously, some extra hours must be available if students are to use the learning center on an unscheduled basis.

Display tables can be used for those study materials which are too bulky or which for some other reason are not included in the booth. Single setup displays, experiments, and demonstrations can be put on the tables. The ideal location seems to be in the middle of the learning center where all students have easy access to them.

Audio-Visual Equipment

There is a definite trend toward using audio tape cassette players rather than reel-to-reel machines. It is the author's recommendation to consider only the cassette format if new equipment is being purchased. However, if your school already has reel-to-reel equipment available for use, you can save the expense of purchasing additional equipment. Preparation of the master tape can be done at the instructor's convenience and should be done on a quality machine. You get what you pay for! Inexpensive playback-only units can be used. The instructor or his assistant can learn to make minor repairs. The machine becomes a disposable item if it is cheaper to replace it rather than fix it.

A variety of projectors are in use in various A-T programs. The 2x2 slide projector is the most commonly used piece of audio-visual equipment other than a tape recorder. Of the various slide projectors, the "carousel" type is the most common. Other slide projectors in use include the "hand-held" single slide viewers, which are fine for a limited number of slides. Very few A-T programs use filmstrip projectors because filmstrips are not as flexible as slides. It is more difficult and expensive to make revisions with filmstrips, since the entire filmstrip has to be re-done, rather than just adding, removing, or switching some slides.

Some A-T lessons are enhanced by the addition of 8mm movies, which permit the inclusion of instruction best done by the use of motion and color. More recently, motion and color are being accomplished by video tape cassettes.

Costs

A cost comparison between Audio-Tutorial and other systems or instructional strategies is impossible to do except when comparing specific situations. Often the question is asked, "How much does it cost to set up an A-T lab?" The answer to that question depends upon whether you want to drive a Volkswagen or a Cadillac. There are relatively inexpensive playback-only tape machines which sell for about twenty dollars when purchased in quantity. At the same time it is possible to spend several hundred dollars for a tape recorder/player. Since only a few students are usually at the same point in their study sequence at the same time, one or two items of equipment, such as microscopes and spectrophotometers, may serve a large number of students. The same is true for films and filmstrips.

Likewise, the amount of staff time required can vary significantly, depending upon the nature of the subject matter, the students, and the instructional situation. Most users of A-T strongly recommend having an instructor available in the learning center whenever the center is open. However, some schools feel that they cannot afford to have a knowledgeable professional available all the time and use para-professionals to assist with the operation of the equipment and to serve as security for the materials and equipment.

Postlethwait states: "High-quality instruction can be given using the Audio-Tutorial system with a low number of staff, but as with conventional systems, the more staff available the more quickly and directly one can meet the specific needs of the students." In other words, the use of the system does not replace the need for the teacher, but does provide the possibility of doing a better job when the total staff available is limited.

Mastery Evaluation

An important part of any learning system is the evaluation phase. Of course, any evaluation strategy can be used with the Audio-Tutorial System. However, the majority of those instructors using the A-T approach use mastery evaluation. Even though a complete treatment of mastery is beyond the scope of this book, let's look at some of its key concepts.

Dr. Benjamin Bloom (1971) states: "Most students (perhaps over 90 percent) can master what we have to teach them, and it is the task of instruction to find the means which will enable our students to master the subject under consideration. Our basic task is to determine what we mean by mastery of the subject and to search for the methods and materials which will enable the largest proportion of our students to attain such mastery." Unfortunately, teachers have been conditioned by the "normal" curve and have come to regard it as a sacred cow in education. The normal curve is designed to detect differences between students, even if the differences are trivial in terms of the content being learned. As a result, failures in a class are often determined by the rank order of the students rather than by their failure to learn the essential ideas of the course. The normal curve is the distribution most appropriate to chance and random activity. Education is a purposeful activity, and we seek to have the students learn what we have to teach. If we are effective in our instruction, the distribution of achievement should be very different from the normal curve. In fact, we may even insist that our educational efforts have been unsuccessful to the extent to which our distribution of student achievement approximates the normal curve.

John Carroll (1963) proposed a strategy for mastery learning. In Carroll's view aptitude is a measure of the amount of time required by the student to attain mastery of a learning task. His assumption is that given enough time all students can conceivably attain mastery of a learning task. The Audio-Tutorial System can provide students the time they need to master the content being studied.

Teachers have for years operated upon the false assumption that there is a standard classroom situation for all students. This standardization is further emphasized by a single textbook for all students in the class. Carroll defines quality instruction in terms of the degree to which the presentation, explanation, and ordering of elements of the task to be learned approach the optimum for a given learner. The quality of instruction is to be considered in terms of its effect on individual learners rather than on a random group of students. The A-T System provides a variety of approaches to meet the needs of different types of students.

In most courses at the high school and college level there is a single teacher and a single set of instructional materials. If the student has facility in understanding the teacher's communications about the learning and the instructional materials (usually a textbook), he or she has little difficulty in learning the subject. If the student has difficulty in understanding the teacher's instruction and/or the instructional materials, he or she is likely to have great difficulty in learning the subject. The ability to understand instruction may be defined as the ability of the learner to understand the nature of the task to be learned and the procedures to be followed in the learning of the task. Again, A-T by its multisensory approach aids each student in understanding the instruction.

If a student needs to spend a certain amount of time to master a particular task, and he spends less than this amount in active learning, he is not likely to learn the task to the level of mastery. Perseverance is related to attitudes toward and interest in learning. Students approach different learning tasks with different amounts of perseverance. The student who gives up quickly in his efforts to learn an academic subject may persevere an unusually long time in learning how to repair an automobile or in learning to play a musical instrument. It would appear that as a student finds the effort rewarding, he is likely to spend more time on a particular learning task. If, on the other hand, the student is frustrated in his learning, he will in self-defense reduce the amount of time he devotes to learning. While the frustration level of students may vary, all students must sooner or later give up a task if it is too painful for them.

Bloom (1971) has found that the demands for perseverance may be sharply reduced if students are provided with the instructional resources most appropriate for them. Frequent feedback accompanied by specific help as needed from the teacher or peers can reduce the time and perseverance required. Improvement in the quality of instruction may reduce the amount of perseverance necessary for a given learning task. There seems to be little reason to make learning so difficult that only a small proportion of the students can persevere to mastery. Endurance and unusual perseverance may be appropriate for long distance running, but they are not great virtues in their own right. The emphasis should be on learning, not on vague ideas of discipline and endurance.

Throughout the world, schools are organized to give group instruction with definite periods of time allocated for particular learning tasks. A course in history at the secondary level may be planned for an academic year of instruction, another course may be planned for a semester, while the amount of instructional time allocated for a subject like arithmetic at the fifth grade level may be fixed. Whatever the amount of time allowed by the school and the curriculum for particular subjects or learning tasks, it is likely to be too much for some students and not enough for other students. The time spent on learning is the key to mastery. Carroll's basic assumption is that aptitude determines the rate of learning and that most, if not all, students can achieve mastery if they devote the amount of time needed to the learning. This implies that the student must not only devote the amount of time he needs to the learning task but also that he be allowed enough time for the learning to take place.

If we are able to develop mastery learning in students, we must be able to recognize when students have achieved it. We must be able to define what we mean by mastery, and we must be able to collect the necessary evidence to establish whether or not a student has achieved it. The specification of the objectives and content of instruction is one necessary precondition for informing both teachers and students about the expectations. The translation of the specifications into evaluation procedures helps to further define what it is that the student should be able to do when he or she has completed the course.

As a rule today, many teachers resistant to change believe that the one-to-one relationship between student and teacher is unrealistic, uneconomical, and impractical. Many teachers claim that they do not have the time or energy to personalize instruction. Further, some teachers argue that the time honored process of lecturing with some discussion is still the best way to teach—it certainly is the predominant means of instruction today.

More traditional teachers normally use the bell-shaped curve, which condemns most of the class to mediocrity. It would be wise to stress mastery of the material; and if the entire class should reach the level of mastery, all of them should earn A! If teaching/learning is to be a humanitarian/ personalized process, why should a depersonalized rule such as the bell-shaped curve become the measure of the students' achievement and success? The learner should be at the very center of what the teacher does, and the role of the teacher ought to be to facilitate the learning of each and every student.

References
(DESIGN FORMAT section)

Bloom, B.S., J.T. Hastings and G.F. Madaus. *Formative and Summative Evaluation of Student Learning.* New York: McGraw-Hill, 1971.

Carroll, J. B. A Model of School Learning. *Teachers College Record*, 1963, *64*:723-733.

Novak, Joseph D. *et. al. The World of Science Series.* Indianapolis: Bobbs-Merrill Company, 1966.

IV.

OUTCOMES

Audio-Tutorial Research

An often asked question about any instructional method is *"Who* learns *what* under what *conditions* in how much *time* and with how much change in *attitude?"* In looking at the question of achievement, Fisher and MacWhinney* reviewed 24 comparative studies. Sixteen of the studies found the A-T method to be superior to "the conventional method" in producing student achievement as measured by a final examination. Eight reported no significant differences, which meant that A-T was just as effective as the other method. None found the conventional lecture to be superior to A-T in promoting achievement. Thus, it can be said that for student achievement on written examinations the A-T method nearly always equals, and usually exceeds, the conventional lecture method.

Fisher and MacWhinney report that the most extensively documented characteristic of A-T instruction is its favorable evaluation by students. When researchers have asked students whether they prefer A-T instruction to conventional instruction, roughly 85 percent of the students state that they prefer A-T instruction. For example, Edwards (1969) found that

*Based upon the excellent review of the literature by Kathleen M. Fisher and Brian MacWhinney reported in *Audio-Visual Communication Review*, 1976, 24:229-261.

the majority of students enjoyed the freedom provided by
the individualization of the A-T approach. Short (1970)
and Hoffman and Druger (1971) found no significant differences in attitudes toward the subject matter between students in A-T and conventional classes, even though students
demonstrated clearly positive attitudes toward the A-T
method of instruction.

Research on A-T has examined the cost-efficiency of the
system. Most of these studies attribute economic advantages
to the A-T method, but the studies point out also that the
initial expenditures required for A-T instruction are relatively
high. It usually requires use of the system for several years to
realize these economic advantages, due to the high initial
cost of the system.

Several studies have examined student reactions to the
various components of the A-T System. Group discussion
sessions received the highest rating of the components in a
study by Becker and Shumway (1972). Husband (1970)
reported that the GAS received the lowest rating of all the
A-T components examined. On the other hand, in an A-T
class which was operating without a GAS, Gelinas (1969)
found that 52 percent of the students would have liked to
have had a lecture provided.

Another series of research studies attempted to determine factors which would predict a student's achievement
in A-T instruction. Diederich and Macklin (1973) found that
students with high SAT math scores and high pretest scores
did significantly better in conventional instruction than A-T
instruction. Students with low SAT math scores and
low pretest scores did significantly better with A-T in a
physics course. They hypothesize that the greater individualization provided by A-T instruction benefits lower-ability
students, while the increased hours of recitation sections in
the conventional treatment benefit higher-ability students.

Szabo and Feldhusen (1971) observed that scores on the restraint scale of the Guilford-Zimmerman Temperament survey did positively correlate with achievement in A-T instruction. Their data shows that high restraint (the tendency to be serious-minded and responsible) was present among those with high achievement. They also observed that among high achievers, prior achievement in mathematical reasoning skills and social studies correlated with success in the conventional course, while prior achievement in mathematics computational skills and science achievement were related to success in the A-T course. This suggests that high achievers with low verbal aptitude and low restraint should learn more under A-T instruction than under more conventional conditions.

In summarizing their review of the research on Audio-Tutorial instruction, Fisher and MacWhinney state: "Student achievement on written examinations with audio-visual, audio-tutorial (A-T) instruction nearly always equals, and usually exceeds, that obtained with the conventional method of instruction. These findings were obtained in 42 out of 43 comparative studies of student achievement. The single most striking observation from this review is the cumulative evidence to suggest that A-T instruction may often be more effective than the lecture method in producing student achievement." They also found that student attitudes toward A-T instruction were strongly positive. On the average, 85 percent of the students enrolled in A-T courses preferred the A-T method of instruction to the lecture method. The characteristics of A-T instruction most valued by students are self-pacing, independent study, group study, and mastery grading. Self-pacing may enhance achievement as well as attitude. Student control of the learning environment appears to be a key element in A-T instruction.

Let's look in detail at one research study dealing with the affective and cognitive achievement of students in an Audio-Tutorial course in World Civilizations (Schnucker, 1974). The experiment was designed to determine the answers to the following questions. When comparing a traditionally taught class and an Audio-Tutorial class teaching the same content:

1. Is there a significant difference between the two courses in the gain of post-test over pre-test scores?
2. Is there a significant difference in the student evaluations of the two courses?
3. Is there a significant difference in the attitudinal changes of the students toward the subject of history?

The experiment was conducted at Northeast Missouri State University in Kirksville. Much of the design of the experiment was determined by the university's curriculum requirements and course registration procedures. Consequently, the instructors had little or no control over the size and student composition of the classes. Thus, the students in the experimental and control groups were not randomly selected for the experiment. However, both classes came from the same population.

At the beginning of the semester both classes were about equal in size (140 in the traditionally taught class and 145 in the A-T section). Both instructors used the same pre-test, the same text, and the same post-test and evaluative instruments. The A-T section had a lower mean score on the pre-test than the traditionally taught class. Further, the traditionally taught group was more positive toward the subject of history than the A-T section at the beginning of the semester, based upon a common pre-test.

The traditionally taught (TT) section met three times per week for a 50-minute lecture and some discussion. The students in the TT section were tested six times during the semester through the use of four multiple-choice tests and two essay tests. Attendance was taken and did figure in the grade earned by the student. At the end of the semester, a curve was used for grading purposes and 7.5 percent earned A, 18 percent B, 39 percent C, 13 percent D, 7 percent F, and 15 percent withdrew.

The Audio-Tutorial section met three times during the entire semester, twice at the beginning for instructions and the administration of the pre-tests and once at the end of the semester for the post-test and evaluations. Since the course did not have required attendance, attendance was not figured into the final grade. By the end of the semester, 47 percent earned A, 35 percent B, one percent C, 0 percent D, 0 percent F, and 17 percent withdrew.
withdrew.

In response to the first question, the experiment yielded the following results: The A-T class pre-test mean was 23 out of 100, while the TT class mean was 31 on the same pre-test. The post-test mean was 77 for the A-T class and 56 for the TT section. Those students in the A-T section more than tripled their pre-test score while those in the TT section did not double their score. Thus, in the cognitive domain, the A-T class did significantly better.

Forty-eight questions were answered by the students in an effort to evaluate the courses. The questions covered the method of teaching history used in their section, history as a subject, and other elements relative to the affective domain. Once the responses were tabulated, they were found to be statistically significant at the .001 level. The responses of the A-T section were significantly more positive toward the method of instruction than those of the TT section. More students in the TT section perceived their approach more difficult than those in the A-T section and more A-T students found their approach less difficult than those students in the TT section. Schnucker hypothesizes that the results might be due in part to the fact that when students are succeeding in a class they feel the class is relevant and they find it to be of less difficulty.

The students in the A-T section began the semester with a more negative attitude toward history than those in the TT section; but, by the end of the semester, 40 percent of the A-T students had become more positive and none became more negative. However, in the TT section, 16 percent became more positive while 12 percent actually became more negative toward history.

On the basis of the data collected, Schnucker concluded:

1. The students in the A-T section learned more than those in the TT section.
2. The students in the A-T section gave more positive evaluations of the course than those in the TT section.
3. More of the students in the A-T section who had begun the class with negative attitudes toward history became more positive to the study of history by the end of the course, while those in the TT section tended to retain their pre-course attitudes.

In summary, Schnucker says: "The implications of this study are important for the history profession. The TT sections have a place in the curriculum, but not the dominant place heretofore enjoyed by them. If the purpose of the history course is to learn the facts of history and how to interpret them in a meaningful manner, the A-T approach seems to accomplish this much more effectively than the TT approach. This study shows that A-T can bring about a more positive change toward the study of history than the TT approach. Unless there is a greater positive change in the affective domain at the freshman and sophomore levels, the history profession will probably experience a decline in enrollment at the upper levels of study which will compound an already difficult situation. Thus, A-T ought to become the predominant means of teaching history at least in the early levels of college and university student experience."

References
(OUTCOMES section)

Becker, W. A. and L. K. Shumway. Innovative Methods of Learning in a General Genetics Course. *Journal of Heredity*, 1972, *63*(3), 122-128.

Diederich, M. E. and D. B. Macklin. *A Trait-Treatment Interaction in a College Physics Course.* Unpublished manuscript, Cornell University, 1973.

Edwards, R. K. An Experimental Study in the Teaching of Business Machines Utilizing an Audio-Visual-Tutorial Laboratory Approach with Continuous-Loop Sound Films. (Doctoral dissertation, Michigan State University, 1969.) *Dissertation Abstracts International*, 1970, *31*, 1135A-1136A. (University Microfilms No. 73-16,606.)

Gelinas, D. *Student Reaction to Audio-Tutorial.* Paper presented at the Audio-Tutorial System Conference, Purdue University, Lafayette, Indiana, October, 1969.

Hoffman, F. E. and M. Druger. Relative Effectiveness of Two Methods of Audio-Tutorial Instruction in Biology. *Journal of Research in Science Teaching*, 1971, *8*, 149-156.

Husband, D. D. Analysis of Certain Components of the Audio-Tutorial System of Teaching. (Doctoral dissertation, Syracuse University, 1970.) *Dissertation Abstracts*

International, 1970, *31*, 1643A-1644A. (University Microfilms No. 70-18,669.)

Schnucker, R. V. The Affective and Cognitive Gains Made by Students in an Audio-Tutorial World Civilizations Course Compared with Students Enrolled in a Traditionally Taught World Civilizations Course. ERIC Document 109 992, 1974.

Short, S. H. The Development and Comparative Evaluation of a Course in Basic Nutrition and Food Science Taught by Self-Instruction Methods. (Doctoral dissertation, Syracuse University, 1970.) *Dissertation Abstracts International*, 1971, *3*, 5803A-5804A. (University Microfilms No. 71-10,981.)

Szabo, M. and J. F. Feldhusen. Success in an Independent Study Science Course at the College Level as Related to Intellective, Personality, and Biographical Variables. *Journal of Research in Science Teaching*, 1971, *8*, 225-229.

V.

DEVELOPMENTAL GUIDE

The Design and Selection of Audio-Tutorial Materials*

Step 1. *Identify Content and Sources of Material*

First the content of the A-T lesson must be determined. It is important to keep the amount of content within reason —usually the amount of information, skills, etc., which the student can master in about an hour. One technique is to start with the content for an entire semester's course and then determine how the content can be broken down into appropriate units.

The source of the course content may be a textbook, reference materials, or one's previous information and knowledge. If the instructor chooses not to use a specific text, he may refer the students to a selected reading list, or he may choose to supply the necessary printed information in the form of handouts or study guides. The most challenging problem is limiting the content to a manageable amount, for both teacher and students.

Step 2. *State Objectives for Each Lesson*

After the content has been identified and delimited, the objectives are stated. The objectives should be stated in the format recommended by Robert Mager (1962) and should

*See Figure 6.

Figure 6

*Steps in the Design
of Audio-Tutorial Materials*

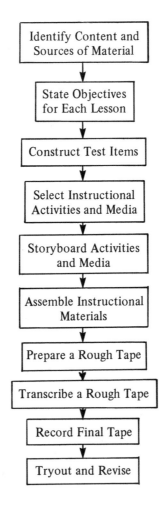

include a performance term, the given conditions and materials, and a statement of minimum acceptable performance.

Each lesson should have a set of objectives which states as specifically as possible the expected performance of the student at the completion of that lesson. The objectives are usually included at the beginning of the study guide or on a separate sheet of paper. Objectives direct the student's attention to the key points within the lesson.

Step 3. *Construct Test Items*

After the objectives have been stated, it is a relatively easy, but important, task to construct the test items or situation which will be used to determine if the student has mastered the content of the A-T lesson. Frequently, evaluation is little more than a restatement of the objectives in question format. Often, alternate forms of the test items can be included in the study guide as a self-check for the student, thereby allowing him to evaluate his own mastery of the lesson content. The student should have ample opportunity during instruction to practice the expected behaviors.

Step 4. *Select Instructional Activities and Media*

Once the content and objectives have been determined, the instructional activities and media can be selected to present the content. It is very helpful to list on individual cards (or small pieces of paper) all the activities and media which might be useful in assisting the students to master the content and objectives for the lesson. Activities might include paragraphs to be read, exercises to be completed, specimens or equipment to be examined, and problems to be solved. Possible media could be written materials, photographs, slides, films, models, etc. When possible a variety of media should be used to provide a multiplicity of sensory input and to help maintain interest.

Step 5. *Storyboard Activities and Media*

By placing each instructional activity and medium on a separate card or sheet of paper, one can manipulate, shuffle, add, discard, etc., with a minimum of organizational effort. The cards are then arranged in a teaching sequence with some activities assigned to the GAS and others to the ISS. The set of cards (storyboard) allows one to examine the entire unit of study or lesson at a glance. These can be readily shifted about until the best activities and media have been selected and the optimum sequence has been decided upon.

Step 6. *Assemble Instructional Materials*

The developer then prepares and assembles the necessary instructional materials—equipment for experiments, visuals, films, real objects, slides, and printed material, including a rough copy of the student study guide.

To prepare the initial draft of the study guide, the first step is to divide the lesson into segments which closely follow a logical arrangement of the objectives. These usually serve as the main headings within the study guide. The body of the study guide should consist of an outline of the lesson. Under each main heading of the outline should appear the exercises or activities which involve the student and determine his or her comprehension of the content. The study guide usually contains little in the way of printed instruction. There should be ample blank space under each heading for note-taking. A glossary of terms and references for additional study are often included at the end of the study guide.

Step 7. *Prepare a Rough Tape*

With the instructional materials and study guide, the developer sits down with a tape recorder and imagines that he is talking with a student, tutoring him or her through the A-T lesson. Don't write a script, but talk your way through the content with the aid of notes. When preparing the audio tape, actively *involve* the student in learning. When possible have him or her looking at diagrams, tables or slides, manipulating real objects, materials or equipment, or recording data. Avoid just having him or her passively listen. The purpose of the tape should be to *investigate* the subject matter with the student. Don't tell the subject to him or her. The tape should *not* be a lecture! Instead the tape should serve to program the activities that the student will perform. When referring to the study guide, a textbook or slides, be sure to orient the student to what you will be talking about *before* you begin talking about it. Then tell the student what to look for. Direct his or her investigation.

When recording the tape, talk naturally. Imagine that you are talking to an individual student. If you desire, a student could be present while you are recording to provide immediate feedback to you on the effectiveness of the presentation. When appropriate, recorded sounds other than voices, voices of outstanding people, and short dialogues provide variety and add realism to the study.

It is helpful to establish a standard set of cues to be used to signal the student when you want him or her to perform a function. A beep or tone, such as striking a spoon on a water glass, or a door chime, can tell the student when to stop the tape, advance the slides, etc. A short interlude of recorded music (approximately ten seconds) can be used to provide a cue that the recorder is to be stopped while the student does an instructional activity or completes a self-check of progress.

Make it clear to the student that he or she can stop and start the tape recorder at will, repeating portions of the instruction as often as is required. Even though some review should be designed into the self-study materials, repetition can be achieved by the individual student through a replay of the appropriate tape segment. Therefore, repetition by the tape narrator is usually unnecessary.

Step 8. *Transcribe Rough Tape*

The rough tape is then transcribed by a secretary. The transcript allows you to correct faulty grammar, to avoid needless repetition, and to clarify confusing statements. The revised transcript serves as a script for the final tape.

Step 9. *Record Final Tape*

Most people find that it is easiest to make the final tape from a script (revised in previous step). Emphasis marking and key ideas can be highlighted on the script.

Step 10. *Tryout and Revise*

The final tape and other materials, including the study guide, are then assembled and used with students. The tryout can provide valuable feedback about the strengths and weaknesses of the Audio-Tutorial lesson. After trying the material with a number of students, you are then in a position to make any necessary revisions of the materials.

It should be emphasized that the development process just described is a *dynamic* one. For more detail on the steps, see Russell (1974). Even though it is represented here as a step-by-step sequence, it is in reality a continuous process. One is not expected to rigorously complete the procedure one step at a time; rather, use the recommended developmental sequence as a guideline—knowing that the A-T lesson should go through all of these steps before it is completed. Developmental activities are highly interactive, with each step having effects on the preceeding steps as well as those which follow it.

If an instructor does not wish to design his or her own Audio-Tutorial materials, some commercially available materials might be found. There are certain factors which should be evaluated before adopting A-T lessons from a commercial publisher. Ideally, the materials should be tried out with the students who will be using them. The suitability of any A-T lesson to any group of students depends upon the relevance of its subject matter, the complexity of the content, and the time required to complete it. In addition, the prerequisites for the lesson should be considered. When examining potential materials, ask questions such as those given in Figure 7.

Six Factors for Success with Audio-Tutorial Systems

1. *Use of Specific Objectives.* The exact specification of instructional objectives is the most important factor in the success of A-T instruction. The design of successful instructional materials with an appropriate selection of audio, visual, printed, and real materials requires clearly stated objectives. Objectives aid the teacher in designing A-T lessons and facilitate student learning during instruction.

2. *Avoid Lecture-on-tape.* When preparing audio tapes imagine you are talking to an individual student and *not* lecturing in a class. The tape should be done in a conversational tone and incorporate simultaneous direct experience with study materials. Prolonged talking by the teacher is boring when live; on audio tape, the lecture can be a "verbal sleeping pill." Keep the student involved in the learning process.

3. *Use Actual Materials.* Whenever practicable, actual materials being discussed or analyzed should be available to students. These real materials provide for active student involvement in the learning sequence and give him practical experience handling specimens, manipulating equipment, performing experiments, and perfecting procedures.

Figure 7

Checklist for Evaluating Audio-Tutorial Materials

Objectives
Are the objectives for the lesson stated in specific behavioral terms with student performance, performance conditions, and acceptable performance standards clearly identified?

Student Population
Is the lesson accompanied by a description of the intended students?
Is the lesson appropriate for the students?
Do the students meet the necessary prerequisites?

Content
Is the treatment of the subject matter accurate and up-to-date?
Are the organization and instructional sequence clear and logical?
Are the learning activities correlated with the objectives so the student can practice that which he is expected to learn?

Media
Does the lesson use a variety of media (visuals, audio tapes, printed materials, films, and actual objects)?
Does the student have the opportunity to use as many senses as possible (visual, audio, tactile, smell, and taste)?
Are real materials handled by the student whenever possible?

Evaluation
Are self-checks included in the lesson so the student can check his own progress?
Is the final evaluation (post-test) correlated with the stated objectives?

4. *Incorporate a Variety of Learning Activities*. In addition to instruction in learning carrels, the A-T lesson should provide students with a variety of meaningful learning experiences. Possible alternatives include demonstrations, experimentation, small-group discussion sessions (with or without supervision), and planned field trips. Discussions with the instructor and other students and evaluative feedback are essential so that each student knows the extent to which he is mastering the objectives of the lesson.

5. *Provide for Student Self-Pacing*. Audio-Tutorial instruction can provide for varying rates of learning. Students who have good subject-area backgrounds and aptitudes will learn new information *several times* more rapidly than students with weaker backgrounds and lower aptitudes. When preparing A-T lessons, you should provide opportunities for the student to check his progress and understanding of the material. If necessary, he should be encouraged to repeat the portion of the lesson causing difficulty or to pursue alternative learning sequences.

The principal source of information for proper pacing of instructional sequences should be student feedback during initial use of the materials. When many students report that they had to repeat a certain portion of an A-T lesson, modify the pace of the instruction, and/or provide more examples of the same concept. Conversely, some segments of the A-T lesson may have unnecessary redundancy, and time as well as motivational gains can result from careful "pruning."

6. *Provide Frequent Feedback and Evaluations*. The design of successful A-T lessons requires continuous monitoring of student progress. Evaluation and feedback can assist students by helping them identify where they are having difficulty and provide suggestions for overcoming the difficulty. One of the best methods for providing feed-

back is to use small (six to ten students) discussion sessions. When instructional objectives are used, peer interaction alone can provide highly valuable feedback to students.

References
(DEVELOPMENTAL GUIDE section)

Mager, R. F. *Preparing Instructional Objectives*, Palo Alto, Calif: Fearon Publishers, 1962.

Russell, J. D. *Modular Instruction*. Minneapolis: Burgess, 1974.

VI.

RESOURCES

BOOKS

Postlethwait, S. N., J. Novak and H. T. Murray, Jr. *The Audio-Tutorial Approach to Learning* (3rd ed.). Minneapolis: Burgess, 1972.

Russell, James D. *Modular Instruction*. Minneapolis: Burgess, 1974.

APPLICATIONS

The Audio-Tutorial Approach is used predominately in the sciences, particularly in biology (botany), where it got its start. However, A-T has been used successfully in all major disciplines, from preschool through graduate school and adult education. Non-academic applications include the military, business and industry, inservice training, and religious education.

PROFESSIONAL ASSOCIATION

International Congress for Individualized Instruction (formerly: International Audio-Tutorial Congress). Membership is $7.00 per year which includes *One-to-One* newsletter. For membership, or more information, contact:

> Dr. John Zimmerman
> Division of Biology
> Kansas State University
> Manhattan, Kansas 66506

CONSULTANTS AND ADDITIONAL INFORMATION
Dr. S. N. Postlethwait
Department of Biological Sciences
Purdue University
West Lafayette, Indiana 47907

Dr. James D. Russell
Department of Education
Purdue University
West Lafayette, Indiana 47907

James D. Russell is Associate Professor of Media Science, Purdue University, West Lafayette, Indiana. Dr. Russell has worked closely with S.N. Postlethwait and the Audio-Tutorial concept during the past eight years. He is the author of *Modular Instruction* (Burgess Publishing, Minneapolis, 1974). In addition to teaching the introductory media course, Dr. Russell is an instructional development consultant for the Laboratory for Applications of Remote Sensing, a research lab at Purdue. As a former high school math and science teacher, he has a breadth of experience in teaching and designing instructional programs. His consulting specialties include instructional uses of media, educational systems technology, the minicourse concept, program design, development, and validation, in addition to the Audio-Tutorial System.